Swing With A Band

Music Minus One

3973

SUGGESTIONS FOR USING THIS MMO EDITION

We HAVE TRIED to create a product that will provide you an easy way to learn and perform these compositions with a full ensemble in the comfort of your own home. The following MMO features and techniques will help you maximize the effectiveness of the MMO practice and performance system:

Because it involves a fixed accompaniment performance, there is an inherent lack of flexibility in tempo. We have observed generally accepted tempi, and always in the originally intended key, but some may wish to perform at a different tempo, or to slow down or speed up the accompaniment for practice purposes; or to alter the piece to a more comfortable key. You can purchase from MMO specialized CD players & recorders which allow variable speed while maintaining proper pitch, and vice versa. This is an indispensable tool for the serious musician and you may wish to look into purchasing this useful piece of equipment for full enjoyment of all your MMO editions.

We want to provide you with the most useful practice and performance accompaniments possible. If you have any suggestions for improving the MMO system, please feel free to contact us. You can reach us by e-mail at *info@musicminusone.com.*

Music Minus One

3973

Contents

COMPLETE VERSION TRACK	MINUS VERSION TRACK		PAGE
	12	Tuning	
1	13	Don't Be That Way...	4
2	14	I'm Through With Love...	8
3	15	Rose Room	10
4	16	I'll Never Be The Same..	12
5	17	How Am I To Know	16
6	18	Stompin' At The Savoy...	18
7	19	I Understand	21
8	20	What Can I Say After I Say I'm Sorry	23
9	21	I'm In The Mood For Love	26
10	22	I Got It Bad (And That Ain't Good)	28
11	23	One O'Clock Jump..	30

TROMBONE

DON'T BE THAT WAY

Benny Goodman, Mitchell Parish
and Edgar Sampson

DON'T BE THAT WAY
Words and Music by Benny Goodman, Mitchell Parish and Edgar Sampson
Copyright ©1938 by Robbins Music Corporation
Rights for the U.S. Extended Renewal Term Controlled by Ragbag Music Publishing Corporation (ASCAP),
Parmit Music and EMI Robbins Music Corporation
All Rights for Ragbag Music Publishing Corporation Administered by Jewel Music Publishing Co., Inc. (ASCAP)
International Copyright Secured   All Rights Reserved   Used by Permission

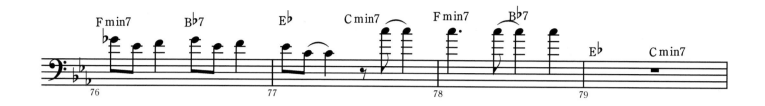

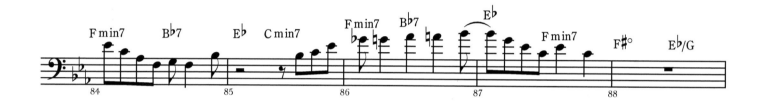

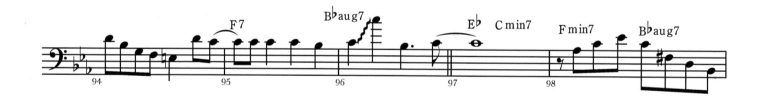

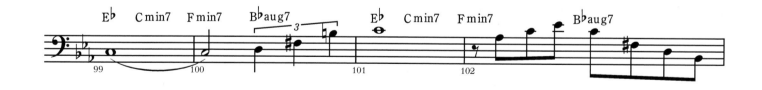

I'M THROUGH WITH LOVE

Gus Kahn, Matt Malneck and Bud Livingston

Moderately, with feeling

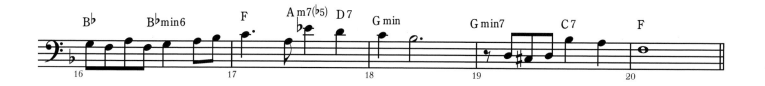

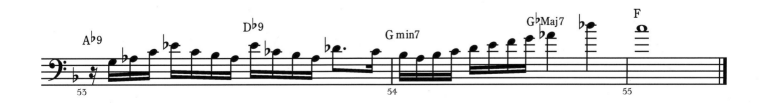

MMO 3973

ROSE ROOM

Harry Williams and Art Hickman

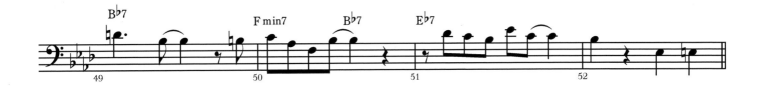

D.S. al Coda

I'LL NEVER BE THE SAME

Gus Kahn, Matt Malneck and Frank Signorelli

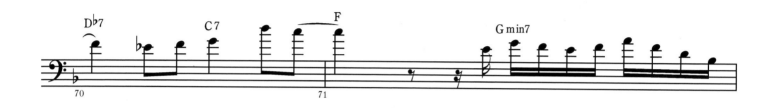

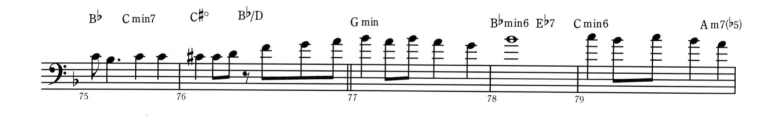

HOW AM I TO KNOW?

Dorothy Parker and Jack King

STOMPIN' AT THE SAVOY

Benny Goodman, Edgar Sampson, Chick Webb
and Andy Razaf

STOMPIN' AT THE SAVOY
Words by Andy Razaf
Music by Benny Goodman, Edgar Sampson and Chick Webb
Copyright ©1936 by EMI Robbins Catalog Inc.
Copyright Renewed by Rytvoc, Inc., Ragbag Music Publishing Corporation (ASCAP), EMI Robbins Music Corporation and Razaf Music Co.
This arrangement Copyright ©2008 by Rytvoc, Inc., Ragbag Music Publishing Corporation (ASCAP),
EMI Robbins Music Corporation and Razaf Music Co.
International Copyright Secured   All Rights Reserved   Used by Permission

I UNDERSTAND

Kim Gannon and Mabel Wayne

MMO 3973

WHAT CAN I SAY
AFTER I SAY I'M SORRY

Walter Donaldson and Abe Lyman

WHAT CAN I SAY AFTER I SAY I'M SORRY
Words and Music by WALTER DONALDSON and ABE LYMAN
© 1926 MILLER MUSIC CORPORATION
Copyright Renewed and Assigned to EMI MILLER CATALOG INC. and DONALDSON PUBLISHING COMPANY
Exclusive Worldwide Print Rights for EMI MILLER CATALOG INC.
Controlled and Administered by ALFRED PUBLISHING CO., INC.
All Rights Reserved

MMO 3973

TROMBONE

I'M IN THE MOOD FOR LOVE

Jimmy McHugh and Dorothy Fields

TROMBONE

I GOT IT BAD
(And That Ain't Good)

Duke Ellington and Paul Francis Webster

ONE O'CLOCK JUMP

Count Basie

MUSIC MINUS ONE
50 Executive Boulevard
Elmsford, New York 10523-1325
800-669-7464 (U.S.)/914-592-1188 (International)

www.musicminusone.com
e-mail: info@musicminusone.com